GREAT MOMENTS IN AMERICAN HISTORY

Little Sure Shot

Annie Oakley and Buffalo Bill's Wild West Show

Jennifer Silate

ROSEN CENTRAL

PRIMARY SOURCE™

THE ROSEN PUBLISHING GROUP, INC., NEW YORK

Published in 2004 by The Rosen Publishing Group, Inc.
29 East 21st Street, New York, NY 10010

Editor: Shira Laskin
Book Design: Layla Sun
Photo Researcher: Rebecca Anguin-Cohen

Photo Credits: Cover (left), title page, p. 22 (NS-245), p. 18 (NS-150) Denver Public Library, Western
History Collection; cover (right) illustration © Debra Wainwright/The Rosen Publishing Group; pp. 6,
10, 31 Garst Museum; p. 14 © Bettmann/Corbis; p. 29 Circus World Museum, Baraboo, Wisconsin;
p. 30 Ohio Historical Society; p. 32 Buffalo Bill Historical Center, Cody, W , I.69.1070

First Edition

Publisher Cataloging Data

Silate, Jennifer
  Little Sure Shot : Annie Oakley and Buffalo Bill's Wild West show /
  Jennifer Silate.
  p. cm. — (Great moments in American history)
  Summary: Annie Oakley, a sharpshooter, joins Buffalo Bill's Wild West show and travels around the
  United States and Europe performing her amazing act.
  ISBN 0-8239-4329-1 (lib. bdg.)
  1. Oakley, Annie, 1860-1926—Juvenile literature 2. Shooters of firearms—United States—
  Biography—Juvenile literature 3. Entertainers—United States —Biography—Juvenile literature   4.
  Buffalo Bill's Wild West Show—Juvenile literature   [1. Oakley, Annie, 1860-1926   2.
  Sharpshooters 3. Entertainers   4. Wild west shows   5. Women--Biography] I. Title   II. Series
  2004

  799.3'092—dc21
  [B]   2003-005998

Manufactured in the United States of America

Contents

Preface

During the 1800s, Western adventure shows were a popular form of entertainment. At these shows, there were horseback riders, cattle ropers, and sharpshooters that performed amazing acts with guns. Most sharpshooters were men—most, but not all.

Annie Oakley, born Phoebe Ann Mozee in 1860 in Ohio, was a talented sharpshooter. Oakley's father died in 1866 and her family was poor. She was sent to work on a farm to earn money. She learned how to use a rifle to hunt. Oakley earned money for her family and became known as a skilled sharpshooter. She won many shooting contests against men.

In 1881, Oakley competed against a famous shooter named Frank Butler. She won the contest— and Butler's heart. They fell in love and married in 1882. They also started a shooting act together.

Oakley and Butler joined the Sells Brothers Circus in 1884. Oakley became the main act and Butler was her manager. She was a great shot, but still unknown to many people.

Oakley got her chance to shine in 1885. She and Butler had left the circus and they joined Buffalo Bill's Wild West show. It was a very popular outdoor show, started by the famous William "Buffalo Bill" Cody. The show had music, parades, horseback riders that did tricks, and fake battles between Native Americans and cowboys. The Wild West show put Oakley in the spotlight. She earned a lot of money, and the nickname "Little Sure Shot" from the Native American chief, Sitting Bull.

Oakley would go on to become the star of the Wild West show. Yet, before she became a star, she had to prove her talent to the toughest audience of all—Buffalo Bill Cody himself....

This photograph of Oakley was taken in 1892. She was performing in London, England with the Wild West show.

Chapter One

A Day at the Circus

*I*t was December 1883. The Sells Brothers Circus was doing a show in New Orleans, Louisiana. The circus had elephants and clowns, acrobats that flew through the air, and a band that played music. The act onstage was the sharpshooting team of Annie Oakley and Frank Butler. Butler would set up targets for Oakley to shoot. She hardly ever missed them. Oakley had great aim.

Oakley peered over her gun. Oakley and Butler's dog, George, sat several yards away. An apple had been placed on George's head. Oakley aimed her gun and pulled the trigger. *BANG!* The apple exploded into hundreds of pieces. George caught a piece as it fell and ate it. The audience laughed and clapped their hands. Oakley aimed her gun again.

This time her eyes were centered on three bottles that were lined up on the stage. Each bottle had a cork in its top. *BANG! BANG! BANG!*

A cork blew off the top of each bottle. The bottles stood untouched. Oakley smiled and looked into the audience. However, her smile faded when she saw how many empty seats there were. Oakley continued her shooting tricks. She finished her act and gave a happy little kick, just as she always did, before running off the stage.

Oakley was very talented and people loved to watch her shoot. She made it look easy to hit the targets and she was a great performer. She always smiled and had fun while she did her act.

After the show that night, Mr. Sells, the owner of the circus, called all of the performers together. It was raining and everyone gathered under the circus tent for the meeting.

"As you have probably noticed," Sells began, "the seats haven't been full since we got to

New Orleans. All of this rain is keeping people from coming to the show. The circus is losing money, folks."

"What do you plan to do?" asked Butler.

"I'm sorry to have to say this, but in a few weeks we are going to have to close down the show for a while," Sells said. The performers groaned. They would need to find new work.

Oakley pulled Butler aside and said, "It looks like we are going to have to pack our bags again. I don't think there is going to be much work here any time soon. We will have to travel around and do our act at any theater that will have us." Butler hugged Oakley and told her not to worry.

The next day, Butler put an advertisement in the newspaper about their act. He hoped that someone would read it and offer them work. They would finish up with the circus and then travel north to look for a place to perform.

This photograph of Buffalo Bill Cody was taken around the time Oakley joined his show. Buffalo Bill signed the picture and gave it to Oakley as a gift.

10

Chapter Two

The Famous Buffalo Bill

A few weeks later, Oakley and Butler were getting ready for one of their last shows with the Sells Circus. Oakley noticed a tall man walking around the circus. It was the famous Buffalo Bill Cody! His show had come to New Orleans and he was visiting the circus.

Buffalo Bill was a famous actor. He was a symbol of the American West. Before he became an actor, he worked for the U.S. Army. He gathered information about Native Americans in the 1860s, when the United States was at war with them. Buffalo Bill was also a great horseback rider and buffalo hunter. People wrote stories about how many buffalo he killed, which led to his nickname.

The stories about Buffalo Bill and his Western adventures were very popular. One writer turned

them into a play. Buffalo Bill was the star of the play. He spent many years as an actor and learned how to thrill audiences.

In 1883, Buffalo Bill opened his own show, called Buffalo Bill's Wild West. He brought together talented people who could bring the West to life. The show was loud and exciting—and audiences everywhere loved it. They didn't feel like they were watching a show. Everything the audience saw was real and happening right before its eyes.

Cowboys did tricks on horses and had battles with Native Americans. There were guns fired so loud that children had to cover their ears. A band played lively music. There were champion shooters, burning cabins, people roping animals, and Native Americans playing drums. It was a thrilling celebration of the West—and Annie Oakley wanted to be a part of it.

Oakley put down her gun and walked over to Buffalo Bill. "My name is Annie Oakley and I am a sharpshooter. My husband and I have a

wonderful act. I can shoot moving targets, bottles, apples, and just about anything else I aim at!" Oakley said, smiling proudly.

Buffalo Bill nodded and said, "I saw you shooting. You are very good, but I already have enough shooting acts in my show. I'm sorry." He left, and Butler rushed over to see what had happened.

"What did he say?" Butler asked. As Oakley told him, Franklin Smith, a clown in the circus, walked over. He had heard Oakley talking to Buffalo Bill.

"Annie, don't be upset. Buffalo Bill turned you down because he has Captain Bogardus in his show," Smith told her. Oakley felt better. Captain Bogardus was the most famous champion shooter around. As long as *he* was a part of the Wild West show, there really was no room for another sharpshooter.

The circus season ended and Oakley and Butler packed their bags to head north to Ohio, where Butler had lined up a few shows.

Oakley posed for many pictures while she worked for the Wild West show. The pictures were often used in advertisements to get people to come see the show. Here, Oakley posed doing one of her most famous shots. She was able to hit her target by looking in the mirror to line up her gun.

14

Chapter Three

Dear Mr. Cody

Through the spring of 1884, Oakley and Butler performed their act in small shows in different parts of Ohio. It was fine work, but Oakley longed for something better. Then one day in March, she got some incredible news.

Not long after Oakley met Buffalo Bill, the Wild West show steamship that carried the show from place to place crashed on the Mississippi River. The show lost animals, wagons, and a lot of equipment. Captain Bogardus lost all of his guns. The show continued, but Bogardus was unhappy and decided to quit.

When Oakley heard that Bogardus quit, she knew what she had to do. Buffalo Bill would need a new star shooting act. Oakley wrote Buffalo Bill a letter, offering her services as a sharpshooter for

his show. She reminded him that he had seen her shoot in New Orleans and thought she was talented. Oakley explained that she could shoot many kinds of guns—even a shotgun. Women shooters at the time never used shotguns because they were heavy, so this made her very special. Oakley felt she deserved high pay for her act and asked for it in the letter.

Oakley waited with high hopes for Buffalo Bill's response. A week later, she got one.

Dear Ms. Oakley,

I remember you from New Orleans. If I remember correctly you are only about 5 feet tall and cannot weigh more than 110 pounds. The guns we use in the show are 10 pounds each. I don't think you could handle them. I also cannot pay you what you asked for. Times have been rough for my show. I do not think I can take on another costly act. For now, I will have to turn down the offer of your services.

Sincerely,
Buffalo Bill Cody

Oakley immediately sat down to write back to Buffalo Bill. She was not going to give up easily. She knew she could handle the guns, and she knew that she was worth the pay that she was asking. Oakley would just have to prove that to Buffalo Bill.

Dear Mr. Cody,

I know that I can handle the 10-pound guns and I will prove it to you. Let me have a three-day tryout. I can do anything Captain Bogardus could do. I can hit any moving target. Give me this chance to show you and I will not let you down. I look forward to hearing from you.

Thank you,
Annie Oakley

After another week, Oakley got a response from Buffalo Bill. He agreed to the tryout. Oakley and Butler would go to Louisville, Kentucky, the last week of April to prove that Oakley was perfect for the show.

Buffalo Bill's Wild West show was popular in many different countries. This photograph shows the cast members in Rome, Italy in 1890. Buffalo Bill stands on the far left, holding a cane. Oakley is on the far right.

Chapter Four

Annie, Get Your Gun!

Oakley practiced hard for the tryout. She decided to try to break five thousand glass balls, a new record for her. Out of a single set of one thousand glass balls, she broke 984. In total, she shot 4,772 of the five thousand glass balls! Oakley was ready for Buffalo Bill. She and Butler left for Louisville.

Buffalo Bill's Wild West show was held in a large tent. Butler and Oakley arrived early. No one was around except for one man sitting off to the side. Since the place was empty, Oakley decided to practice.

Butler set up a clay bird machine. It sent clay targets flying up into the air. "Ready!" She shouted. Two clay birds flew from their holders. *BANG! BANG!* Oakley pulled her gun's trigger twice and

the birds exploded. Then, Oakley turned her gun upside down. "Ready!" she yelled—three more birds exploded. Oakley continued with the gun in her right hand *and* in her left hand. She shot as fast as she could. As always, she was amazing.

When Oakley finished, she heard clapping. She looked around. It was the man who had been sitting on the side of the tent. He walked toward them, smiling.

"Fantastic!" he yelled. "That's the best shooting I have seen in a long time. What is your name?"

"Thank you, sir. My name is Annie Oakley," replied Oakley.

"I'm Nate Salsbury. I am the business manager for the Wild West show. I'm in charge of hiring acts. How would you like to work for us?" Salsbury said as he shook Oakley's hand.

Oakley was thrilled. "Mr. Salsbury, there is nothing I would like more!" she answered.

"Wonderful! I'll have posters made right away. A woman who can shoot like you is going

to be a big star!" exclaimed Salsbury. Oakley couldn't believe it. She had not even had her tryout and she had the job!

Buffalo Bill and the other performers entered the tent. They had just finished marching in a parade through Louisville to let everyone know that the show was opening that night.

"Bill, come over here!" Salsbury called. "I'd like you to meet your new champion shooter, Annie Oakley. She is even better than Captain Bogardus!"

Buffalo Bill smiled at Oakley. He knew that if Salsbury liked her act, she was really something special. "We have met before. It's nice to see you again, Missie. Welcome to our show," Buffalo Bill said as he took Oakley's hand.

"It's a pleasure for me, too, Mr. Cody," replied Oakley.

Salsbury lined up everyone in the show and introduced Oakley. Then he turned to her and said, "Annie, you better get ready—the show opens tonight!"

BUFFALO BILL'S WILD WEST·
CONGRESS, ROUGH RIDERS OF THE WORLD.

A. Huen & Co., Baltimore, U.S.A.

MISS ANNIE OAKLEY,
THE PEERLESS LADY WING-SHOT.

Buffalo Bill and Nate Salsbury had many posters made to get people to come see their show. This one, from the 1890s, features Oakley in her show costume. In the background, there are other pictures of Oakley shooting glass balls in the sky.

Chapter Five

Little Sure Shot

"Are you nervous?" Butler asked Oakley just before her first show was about to start. "No, just excited!" Oakley replied.

"Well, good luck tonight," Butler said. "I know they are going to love you!" Oakley pinned a star to her hat and put it on her head. She was so happy to be a part of this magical show. Her dream of being in Buffalo Bill's Wild West had finally come true. Oakley excitedly watched from behind the curtain as the opening act began.

The Cowboy Band started playing the "Star-Spangled Banner." A group of Native Americans on horseback tore through the curtain. They had feathers in their hair and their faces were colored with war paint. Cowboys charged out on their

horses, stopping just before the front row of seats in a puff of dust. They cheered and yelled as they rode around the arena, waving their hats in the air. As trumpets played, Buffalo Bill, on his beautiful gray horse, trotted out. The audience was silent, amazed by the excitement of it all.

Everyone stopped as Buffalo Bill screamed, "Are you ready to go?" The performers shouted and whooped loudly, riding around the arena at full speed. Oakley watched while Buffalo Bill and a Native American acted out a fight. When the act was over, the stage was cleared. It was time for Oakley to show everyone what she could do.

Oakley took a deep breath and skipped out into the arena. She smiled, waved, and blew kisses at the audience. Butler appeared next to a table that had glass balls and other objects for Oakley to shoot. She picked up her first gun. She nodded at Butler. He grabbed six glass balls and threw them up into the air. Oakley

took aim and pulled her trigger. One after another, the glass balls broke. The audience cheered. Oakley bowed to the crowd and picked up another gun and a small mirror. Oakley put the gun on her shoulder, aimed behind herself, and held up the mirror to see a card that Butler was holding. Oakley pulled the trigger. *BANG!* Half of the card fell to the ground. The audience exploded with applause. Oakley continued to wow the audience with every trick. Each was more amazing than the next.

Her final trick was the hardest. Oakley had six guns laid out in front of her. Butler threw a glass ball. She picked up a gun and shot it. As soon as the first ball broke, Butler threw two more into the air. Oakley quickly picked up another gun and shot each glass ball. Oakley used all six guns to break eleven glass balls in only 10 seconds. When she finished, Oakley laid down her smoking gun and blew a kiss at the audience. She ran around the arena waving, and did her little kick before dashing through

the curtain. Everyone in the crowd was on their feet. Oakley could hear the applause from backstage. The audience loved her.

Before long, audiences everywhere fell in love with Oakley. She became the star of the show. Her face appeared on posters all over the country. She worked with Buffalo Bill's Wild West show for seventeen years. She traveled around the United States and Europe performing her act. Newspapers told of her amazing tricks and people traveled from many places to watch her shoot. Oakley never cheated, which was something that a lot of sharpshooters at that time did. She rarely missed her mark because she was so talented with a gun.

Oakley became a Western legend. She was America's greatest female sharpshooter. Oakley became famous doing something that people thought only men could do. Many of those men had to cheat to look good, but not Oakley. She was Little Sure Shot.

Glossary

advertisement (ad-ver-TISE-muhnt) a public notice, usually published in the press or broadcast over the air, that calls attention to something, such as a product or an event

arena (uh-REE-na) a large area that is used for sports or entertainment

audience (AW-dee-uhnss) the people who watch or listen to a performance, speech, or movie

champion (CHAM-pee-uhn) the winner of a competition or a tournament

curtain (KURT-uhn) a piece of fabric pulled across a window or stage to cover it

manager (MAN-uh-jur) someone in charge of a store, business, etc., or in charge of a group of people at work

sharpshooter (SHARP-shoo-tur) someone who is very skilled at shooting a gun

symbol (SIM-buhl) a design or an object that represents something else

target (TAR-git) a mark, circle, or object that is aimed or shot at

trigger (TRIG-ur) the lever on a gun that you pull to fire it

Primary Sources

We can learn about Annie Oakley's life and the time in which she lived by looking for clues. These clues can be found in sources such as old letters, diaries, paintings, maps, and photographs. For example, the letter on page 31 helps us draw the conclusion that Buffalo Bill and Oakley were close friends. In the letter, Buffalo Bill wrote about how sad he was to read a French newspaper story about Oakley's death. He also thanked her for a Christmas card she sent him. By reading this letter, we learn that Buffalo Bill trusted Oakley as his friend.

Primary sources also help us reconstruct parts of Oakley's life. Oakley used the trunk shown on page 32 when she traveled in Europe with the Wild West show. On these trips, Oakley often used the trunk as her dresser because of its special shape. Sources such as Buffalo Bill's letter and Oakley's trunk give us clues to learn about Oakley's life.

This 1883 photograph of Butler and Oakley features their poodle, George. Often, George was an important part of their sharpshooting act. Oakley would shoot different objects off of his head.

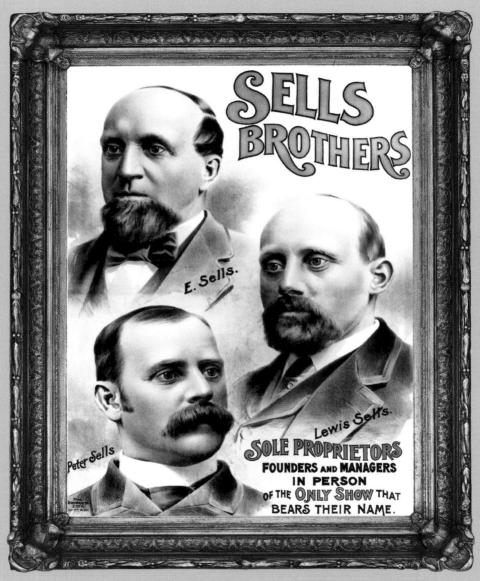

This poster for the Sells Brothers Circus features the show's owners, Ephriam (top), Lewis (middle), and Peter (bottom). Although the circus went through hard times, it was successful at times as well. At its best, the circus had over three hundred workers and fifty cages of wild animals.

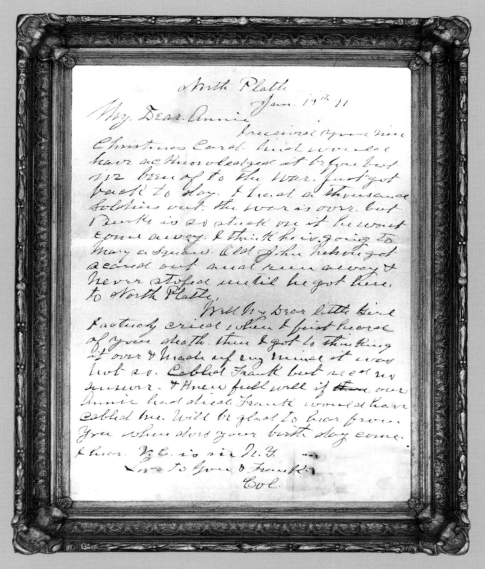

Buffalo Bill wrote this letter to Oakley on January 19, 1891. In it, he wrote, "the war is over." The war he spoke of is the years of fighting between white settlers and Native Americans. Buffalo Bill's friend, the Sioux Indian chief Sitting Bull, was killed in December 1890. Buffalo Bill knew Sitting Bull's death would lead to the end of the war.

Oakley used this trunk to carry her costumes when she traveled with the Wild West show. Because the bottom drawers were so long, Oakley didn't have to fold her dresses. This kept them neat for each new show.